EZEKIEL

FOR HIS GLORY

10 Publishing
a division of 10 of those.com

First published in Great Britain in 2014

British Library Cataloguing in Publication Data
A record for this book is available from the British Library

ISBN: 978-1-909611-83-2

Designed by Diane Bainbridge
Printed in the UK

10Publishing, a division of 10ofthose.com
9D Centurion Court, Farington, Leyland, PR25 3UQ, England
Email: info@10ofthose.com
Website: www.10ofthose.com

Peter Lau

49 UNDATED DEVOTIONS THROUGH THE BOOK OF EZEKIEL

DAY 1

READ Ezekiel 1:1–3

Have you ever been far from home? How did you feel?

As the book of Ezekiel opens we find that a group of Israelites have been exiled from home (v. 1). The might of the Babylonian army had attacked Jerusalem in 598 BC and forcibly deported the elite, the leaders. We're told that King Nebuchadnezzar dragged away the king and his family, the palace officials, the fighting men, the craftsmen and metalworkers: that is, all the people most useful to build the Babylonian Empire (see 2 Kgs 24:10–16). Removing them also removed the threat of an uprising. Ezekiel was among those banished, and as the word of the LORD comes to him, the exiles had been away from home for five years (v. 2). How do you think they would have felt?

Psalm 137 captures some of their emotions.

1 By the rivers of Babylon we sat and wept when we remembered Zion. ... 3 there our captors asked us for songs, our tormentors demanded songs of joy; they said, 'Sing us one of the songs of Zion!' 4 How can we sing the songs of the LORD while in a foreign land?

So the exiles were in despair. They were far away from their temple and their land. They were probably wondering, 'Has our God, the LORD, been defeated by the Babylonian gods?' And they were also probably anxiously thinking, 'Has God abandoned us?' We'll see God's response to these types of questions in the next devotion.

For now, also spare a thought for Ezekiel. Since he came from a family of priests, for all his life he'd been groomed to follow in his father's footsteps (vv. 1-3). The usual age to begin priestly duties was thirty years old (cf. Num. 4:3). But when Ezekiel turned thirty, instead of beginning ministry as a priest, God calls him to be a prophet, His mouthpiece. How will Ezekiel respond? More importantly, how will the exiles respond to God's word spoken to them through the prophet? We'll find out as we study the book of Ezekiel together.

DAY 2

READ Ezekiel 1:4–28

What a spectacular opening to the book of Ezekiel! Thunderbolts and lightning; very, very frightening creatures. By the Kebar Canal in Babylon Ezekiel finds himself swept up in a weirdly wonderful vision.

What Ezekiel sees in the vision is God's glory, with three main parts:

1. **A windstorm and four living creatures (vv. 1–14)**. The cloud, lightning and fire in the windstorm are reminiscent of God's presence. This windstorm comes from the north (v. 4), the traditional direction from which Israel's enemies attacked. The creatures are almost grotesque. There are four creatures with four faces each (v. 10), probably representing the apex of each type of creature.
2. **Wheels beneath the creatures (vv. 15–21)**. The wheels are within wheels and are studded with eyes.
3. **An expanse and a throne above the creatures (vv. 22–28)**. On the far side of the expanse Ezekiel sees a magnificently bright 'figure like that of a man' (v. 26) on the throne.

What are we to make of this riot of images? Ezekiel tells us that this was 'the appearance of the likeness of the glory of the LORD' (v. 28). The prophet's description of the vision is cluttered and clumsy, because he can't put down in words what he saw. And his final conclusion is vague because, as someone with a priestly background, he just can't come out and say, 'I saw God.' He knows that he can't see God and live (Exod. 33:20). Yet God does reveal something of Himself to Ezekiel by showing limited aspects of His glorious character:

1. **He is different.** The things in the vision are way beyond anything Ezekiel or we have experienced.
2. **He is King of the universe.** He is seated on His mobile throne chariot, able to move anywhere, able to see everything.
3. **He will judge.** God comes from the north to judge His people.

REFLECTION

Do you respond to Jesus, God's ultimate revelation of His glory (e.g. John 1:14), with wholehearted worship, like Ezekiel (v. 28)?

DAY 3

READ Ezekiel 2:1–8

We left Ezekiel at the end of chapter 1 face-down in worship of God. In chapter 2 the prophet is hauled to his feet by God's Spirit and called to present God's message to the people of Israel (vv. 1–2).

Yet the way Israel is described is enough to turn anyone off the task. The rebellious nature of Ezekiel's audience is mentioned seven times in six verses (vv. 3–8). They are stubborn and obstinate, literally 'hard of face' and 'hard of heart/mind'. This is not a one-off condition; it has been going on for generations. Not only is the present generation rebellious but their ancestors also transgressed against God (v. 3).

The spotlight then shifts to Ezekiel (vv. 6–8). Israel might be rebellious by nature but that is not how the prophet is to be. He is described as 'the son of man' or 'human one' (vv. 1, 3, 6, 8), in contrast to God and the heavenly creatures of the opening vision. Ezekiel's audience is hardened and prickly, and they will bring him pain and suffering (v. 6). Nonetheless, he is commanded to listen to and obey God. As the people reject the message Ezekiel gives, they are actually rejecting God's words, God's message (v. 7).

In terms of the stubbornness of hearers, not much has changed, has it? As we present the message of the momentous news of Jesus, the response, sadly, is often still the same. Indeed, the New Testament describes people as darkened and alienated from God because of their ignorance from the hardness of their hearts (Eph. 4:18). As Christians we too were once like this, but are now responsive to God because of the indwelling of the Holy Spirit. Just like Ezekiel, we can now obey God. As we present God's message of the ultimate 'Son of Man' who suffered for our sake, we know that not all will take to it positively. Thus the faithfulness of our ministry cannot be measured by numerical response.

REFLECTION

Is this your experience as you share the gospel? What encouragement does this passage give you to persevere?

DAY 4

READ Ezekiel 2:9 – 3:27

The first test of Ezekiel's obedience comes in this passage (2:9 – 3:3). The prophet is shown a scroll, filled on both sides with words of judgement (2:9–10). Ezekiel is then asked to eat the scroll, which he does, and, paradoxically, it tastes sweet (3:1–3). Even words of woe and gloom are like honey because they are God's words.

God next repeats His call to Ezekiel: to present God's words to His hardened people, words that the prophet has just swallowed (3:4–11). This is a vivid illustration of the prophet's role as God's mouthpiece. The words do not come from the prophet's imagination but come directly from God (cf. Deut. 18:18).

The Spirit then brings Ezekiel back to the rest of the exiles (3:12–15). After all that the prophet has seen, it is not surprising that he is overwhelmed for a whole week (3:15). But it is surprising that he feels bitterness and anger (3:14). Why does he feel like this? It may be because he is infuriated with God's call for his life, or he shares some of the hardness of the people, or he feels God's indignation at the rebellion of the people. Or it may be a combination of all these.

At the end of seven days, God again speaks to Ezekiel to further describe his role (3:16–21). The prophet is to be a watchman, warning of impending danger. Unlike a typical watchman, however, Ezekiel is not stationed in the tower of the city. Instead, he is to give warning of the impending judgement of God because of the peoples' continued sin. Those who choose a life of righteousness will find life; those who choose wickedness will experience death. A watchman may be the prophet's task but then he finds himself restricted, both physically and verbally (3:22–27).

As Christians we too are watch-persons. We must warn of the coming and certain judgement of God against sin and wickedness. We need to urge people to repent. We need to get out there and spread the gospel, because people cannot be saved apart from hearing it (Rom. 10:14).

REFLECTION

How can you sound the alarm as a watchperson among your family and friends?

DAY 5

READ Ezekiel 4

In order to penetrate the hardness of the people, God commands Ezekiel to perform 'sign-acts'. These are actions with a significance beyond themselves, similar to street theatre or church dramas today. But Ezekiel's sign-acts are more than these modern-day analogues because his actions also hold prophetic significance for Israel (v. 3).

The first set of sign-acts is found in chapter 4:

1. The prophet lays siege to a clay brick that has a map of Jerusalem drawn on it (vv. 1–3). In the immediate context, the iron pan most likely represents a barrier in the relationship between God and Israel (cf. 3:26). This prophetic action anticipates the Babylonian army erecting siege works against Jerusalem (cf. 2 Kgs 25:1–2).
2. Ezekiel lies on his left side for 390 days, then his right for 40 days (vv. 4–8). Each day corresponds to a year of Israel and Judah's sin, and Ezekiel is to symbolically bear the people's sin.
3. The prophet is to eat a siege diet and drink rationed water during the time he lays on his side (vv. 9–17). This points to the restricted diet that those in Jerusalem would experience during the siege (cf. 2 Kgs 25:3). Their emaciated state would lead the people to identify the cause of their distress: their sin. Indeed, the wording is reminiscent of the covenant curses for disobedience (cf. Lev. 26:26, 39). For Ezekiel, from a priestly background, it is detestable to eat food cooked over human excrement, so God permits him to cook over cow manure instead. This symbolises the unclean food that God's people would eat in exile.

This set of sign-acts looks forward to the terrible fate of Jerusalem from the hand of God. The judgements of siege, famine and exile to unclean lands are God's punishment for Israel's sin.

REFLECTION

Was Ezekiel effective in bearing and removing Israel's sin? The people still went into exile as punishment, so the answer is 'No.' But thank God for Jesus, who, in the ultimate sign-act of the cross,[1] did away with sin as our substitute (e.g. John 1:29).

DAY 6

READ Ezekiel 5

Ezekiel is asked to perform another sign-act (vv. 1–4). This time he is to cut off the hair on his head and his beard. Of the hair, one third will suffer punishment by fire, one third will be struck by the sword and one third will be scattered in the wind. Yet there is also a hint of mercy: a few strands of hair are to escape both this punishment and a second burning. This points to the fact that a remnant of those in Jerusalem will be spared, although they too will suffer punishment and refinement (v. 4).

Among all the nations, Israel had a privileged position (Exod. 19:5–6). The nation was meant to be the centre of God's purposes for the nations. If they obeyed the law, they would be admired for their wisdom and understanding (Deut. 4:6–8). They were meant to be a showcase nation, revealing God's character to the world and bringing the nations blessing (Gen. 12:1–3). Yet they hadn't lived up to their identity and calling. In fact, their wickedness was judged to be worse than all those around them (vv. 6–7).

God's response to Israel's disobedience will be in the sight of the nations, as a warning to them (v. 8). For an Israelite, it would have been terrifying to hear God say, 'I myself am against you' (v. 8). He declares that He will execute a judgement unlike any in the past and any that will be again (v. 9). This judgement is outlined in specific detail: famine, wild beasts, pestilence and sword (vv. 10–12, 16–17). It encompasses the full house of divine curses for covenant disobedience (cf. Lev. 26:14–39). What will happen to God's people will be a horror and an object lesson for the observing nations (v. 15).

Christians, as the Israel of God (Gal. 6:16), are also to live up to our identity and calling. We too are a chosen people, a holy nation, called to declare God's praises to the nations (1 Pet. 2:9–10).

REFLECTION

We still live in and among an observing world. So we must live according to our identity and calling. Yet we also need to heed the warnings for those who fail in these (Rev 1:9–3:22).

READ Ezekiel 6

After outlining God's judgement against Jerusalem and its inhabitants (Ezek. 5), in this chapter Ezekiel widens his attention to the rest of the land (vv. 1–3). It seems strange that the prophet would prophesy against the mountains, objects that can't hear or respond. But the prophecy is really for the sake of the Israelite hearers, who have used the mountains for their idolatrous worship. Again, the way God's judgement against the false worship is described echoes the threats of punishment for covenant disobedience (vv. 4–7; cf. Lev. 26:30). The amount of disdain that God has for Israel's graven images is reflected in the word for idols: literally 'dung pellets'. It would have been shocking for God's people to hear their objects of worship being described like this, but imagine how offensive it was for God that they would crave after them in the first place.

So Ezekiel is commanded to clap his hands and stomp his feet, to grab the attention of his hearers and to accentuate God's anger towards them (vv. 11–14). A triad of divine judgements is threatened again, with no one to be spared (v. 12). God will stretch out His hand against His people, bringing comprehensive judgement against Israel's idolatrous worship (vv. 13–14).

Nonetheless, God's grace breaks through in the middle of this chapter (vv. 8–10). A remnant will be spared, who, in exile, will realise the effect their idolatrous whoring has on God. They will detest themselves because of their evil ways, and they will repent.

In this chapter we gain a telling insight into God's anguish over Israel's unfaithfulness. In His holiness and justice He must devastate the land and its inhabitants. But we also see that God is crushed and heartbroken because of His people's idolatrous hearts. He's not just a cold-hearted, impassible God.

REFLECTION

As Christians God disciplines and rebukes us because we are His beloved children (e.g. Heb. 12:5–11; Rev. 3:19). Will we respond by remembering God's grace and realise the pain we're causing God? Will we be corrected by God and repent?

DAY 8

READ Ezekiel 7

Despite God's strong message of judgement against Israel, we were still able to find glimpses of God's mercy in the previous chapters. It is hard to find any such hope in this chapter. We can see at least three aspects of God's judgement:

1. **It is imminent**. 'The end' is repeated three times, so we can't miss it, and the end is 'now' (vv. 2–3). God is not going to withhold His judgement this time, and His threat is ominous: 'I will not look on you with pity or spare you' (v. 4).
2. **It is just and personal**. He will punish according to past conduct, especially detestable practices. The personal nature of divine judgement is highlighted by the use of the singular pronoun 'you' (not 'you all'). Each person will be repaid according to the abominations they have committed (vv. 3–4, 8–9). Idolatry is mentioned (e.g. v. 20), along with sins committed against one another, namely bloodshed and violence (v. 23).
3. **It is wide-ranging in its scope and effect**. It involves the whole of the land (vv. 2, 15); no people will be left (v. 11); commercial transactions will shudder to a halt (vv. 10–13, 19); military warfare will be useless (v. 14); and guidance from leadership will fail (v. 26).

What will be the response of the people to this judgement? Some who escape to the mountains may be remorseful and repentant (v. 16). Others will feel shame and mourn (v. 18). Most will 'wet their pants' in fear (v. 17).

This is a terrifying picture of God's comprehensive judgement. There comes a time when God's judgement is all that is left for people, especially if there is sustained, persistent rebellion against Him.

Some popular portrayals of God focus solely on His love and compassion. This chapter balances such a caricature by filling in attributes such as His holiness, justice and wrath.

REFLECTION

God has set a day for the final judgment of all people (Acts 17:31). Let's tell people of God's grace in Jesus Christ, and urge everyone to repent and trust in Him while there is still time.

READ Ezekiel 8

If you go online, you can find virtual tours of potential houses for rent or sale. In this chapter Ezekiel is given another vision, a virtual tour of God's house. It's a tour of the abominations taking place in the temple in Jerusalem, with four locations:

1. **Northern inner court (vv. 1–6).**
   Here is an idol that provokes God to jealousy. Israel was meant to be faithful to God because they were in an exclusive covenant relationship with Him (see Exod. 20:1–6). Instead, they had been unfaithful, and so provoked God to jealousy and anger. Yet there's more.
2. **Entrance to the outer court (vv. 7–13).**
   Ezekiel is asked to dig into the wall and finds a secret entrance. Why so secretive? Because seventy elders are committing vile abominations, worshipping their creepy crawly gods. Their excuse? They claim that God has forsaken them, that God can't see what they are doing. Yet there's more.
3. **North gate of the temple (vv. 14–15).**
   Here the women are involved in mourning the death of a Babylonian god, hoping to speed the return of fertility for crops and livestock. Yet there's more.
4. **Inner court of the temple (v. 16).**
   The last stop is right in the heart of the temple. Here we find twenty-five men with their backs to the temple, worshipping the sun in the east! The men have turned away from God, both literally and symbolically.

So what we see are various acts of spiritual adultery, committed from the front gate of God's house to the master bedroom. Yet there's more. The people's final act of defiance, either another form of false worship or a gesture of insult to God, provokes God to anger (v. 17). Frighteningly, He is implacable in His anger; nothing will stop His judgement (v. 18).

This tour highlights the syncretism in Israel: merged together are Canaanite, Egyptian and Babylonian worship, and perhaps even worship of God. Yet God will not tolerate this 'mix-and-match' religion.

REFLECTION

Do you add other religions or superstitions to your faith? We belong to God alone (1 Pet. 2:9), so we need to be careful not to provoke Him to jealousy (1 Cor. 10:22).

DAY 10

READ Ezekiel 9

This chapter continues Ezekiel's vision which began in the last chapter. God had been provoked to anger, and here He acts in widespread judgement. But His judgement is not indiscriminate.

The loud cry of God summoning the executioners (v. 1) parallels the shouts of the people that God had turned a deaf ear to (8:18). Six of these heavenly beings appear, with weapons for slaughter in their hands. The seventh functions as a scribe, one who marks out the repentant among the people (vv. 1–4).

The executioners are then commanded to carry out God's judgement (5–7). The executioners show no pity, slaughtering men and women, young and old. They begin at the temple, where the elders were worshipping the sun (8:11). The temple had been defiled by idolatrous worship, and is now further defiled by dead bodies.

Seeing this horrific scene, the usually stoical prophet is compelled to intercede on behalf of the remnant of Israel (vv. 8–10). God's reply doesn't sound hopeful: He simply reiterates the people's guilt, and His determination to repay them for their sins. Yet hope is found in the next verse, as the man clothed in linen reports that he has marked out those who would be saved (v. 11).

We rightly think of God as merciful and gracious, slow to anger and abounding in steadfast love (Exod. 34:6). Yet He is also a God of justice, moved in this chapter to such determined, terrifying judgement because of Israel's severe, pervasive and ongoing disobedience. In their life and worship practices, Israel had become just like the Canaanites, so their punishment would be similar (e.g. Gen. 15:16; Deut. 9:4–5).

REFLECTION

Judgement will begin with the house of God (1 Pet. 4:17). We need to take God's judgement seriously for it is not only for non-Christians. But thank God that we will be spared the ultimate judgement, since we too have been marked out (e.g. Rev. 7:3; 9:4; 14:1).

DAY 11

READ Ezekiel 10

In this chapter we find two other aspects of God's judgement because the people had broken the covenant, especially in their adulterous worship practices.

First, Jerusalem is razed to the ground. The city is burned by fire from God Himself, with burning coals taken from below His throne (vv. 1–2). The 'man clothed in linen' from the previous chapter now changes his role from an agent of deliverance to one of judgement (vv. 6–8). The scattering of coals over a city echoes the judgement upon Sodom and Gomorrah (Gen. 19:24); Israel is as deserving of God's judgement as they were.

Second, God departs from the temple. God warned that Israel's abominations would drive Him from His sanctuary (8:6). Here we see it taking place in three halting movements:

1. The glory of the LORD moves from His throne above the tips of the cherubim on top of the ark to the threshold of the temple (9:3).
2. The LORD moves from the threshold of the temple to the south side of the temple, to rest above the cherubim (vv. 3, 18). This 'divine throne chariot' then moves the LORD to the east gate of the temple (v. 19). The throne chariot is the same as the one Ezekiel had seen in the first vision (vv. 20–23).
3. The LORD leaves the temple proper, heading to the mountain to the east of Jerusalem, most likely the Mount of Olives (11:22–23).

This halting departure reflects God's reluctance to leave His house. But He's been driven from it by the abominations committed there by His people.

God's presence with His people, especially dwelling in the temple, was central to Israel's identity and security. Solomon knew that God was not tied to one place, yet God had chosen to place His name there (1 Kgs. 8:27–29; Deut. 12:11). Even when Israel abandoned the covenant, they still clung dearly to the temple (Jer. 7:1–15). Yet now that God has left it, Israel is exposed to destruction.

REFLECTION

As Christians we can praise God that He is present with us by His Holy Spirit, who dwells in us and will be with us forever (John 14:16–17).

This chapter concludes Ezekiel's vision that began in chapter 8. In it we find a foretaste of God's imminent judgement, yet also evidence of God's grace.

Ezekiel is asked to prophesy judgement against the public officials who remained in Jerusalem after the deportation of 597 BC (vv. 1–13). The sentiment in the city is that everything is safe, secure and under control. They are like the meat in a cauldron, protected by the city walls (v. 3), or so they think, but they have another thing coming. Violence they have committed, and violence they will suffer. Indeed, the walls will be no protection, as God will judge them for the sins they have committed (vv. 9–12).

Even as Ezekiel is speaking, one of the leaders drops dead before the prophet's eyes (v. 13). This is a foretaste of God's judgement that will fall upon the leaders and the rest of the people in Jerusalem. Again the generally stoical prophet responds by asking if God is going to destroy the whole remnant (cf. 9:8). God's answer before was implied, but this time it is unambiguous. God will show grace to the exiles in at least four ways (vv. 14–21). He will:

1. Still be with them as their 'sanctuary'.
2. Gather them from distant lands and return them to the Promised Land.
3. Give them a new heart and a new spirit, enabling them to turn away from idolatry and to obey Him.
4. Accept them as His covenant people again (cf. Exod. 6:7; Lev. 26:12).

Just as Ezekiel is given a foretaste of God's imminent judgement (vv. 1–13), he is also asked to present a foretaste of God's future grace in the restoration of Israel (vv. 14–20). This hope is fleshed out in the final section of the book of Ezekiel (chapters 33–48).

Even amid the overpowering message of judgement, God is still faithful to His covenant promises. Even before His judgement has fully begun, He offers a message of hope.

REFLECTION

Thank God for His covenant faithfulness, which extends to us today. All God's promises are 'Yes' in Jesus Christ (2 Cor. 1:20).

DAY 13

READ Ezekiel 12

Ezekiel next presents two dramas and two rebuttals.

The dramas foretell what is going to happen to Jerusalem:

1. Ezekiel digs a hole in the wall of his house and goes through the wall with his baggage, walking off into the distance (vv. 3–7). Although the prophet performs the sign-act in the sight of the people, they do not see; that is, they don't understand (vv. 2, 8–9). So the prophet explains that it symbolises what will happen to the king and the people in Jerusalem (vv. 10–16). King Zedekiah will leave Jerusalem through a hole dug in the wall, but the outcome will be shameful for him for he will be blinded by the Babylonians (2 Kgs. 25:7) and will never see his land again. The people also will be dragged away into exile.
2. Ezekiel eats and drinks with fear, trembling and shaking (vv. 17–18). This symbolises what it will be like for those in Jerusalem during the siege (vv. 19–20). After the siege Jerusalem will be destroyed.

Two rebuttals then follow the dramas:

1. The people have distilled a proverb, asserting that God's prophecies are ineffective and that they won't be fulfilled (vv. 21–25). God refutes their assertion: what He says will be done.
2. The people (perhaps another group) assert that God's prophecies concern the distant future (vv. 26–28). This thinking is understandable, given that many prophecies did concern a time beyond the people. But God refutes this statement: there will be no delay.

So the siege and exile is a coming reality for the people in Jerusalem. God prophesies these events through His prophet. It will certainly happen and it will take place soon.

REFLECTION

We can be certain of God's word; He will do what He says. Jesus teaches that God's judgement is also coming (e.g. Matt. 24:36 – 25:46). We don't know exactly when this will be but we need to live as if it is soon, making sure our lives are in order and warning others of this judgement.

DAY 14

READ Ezekiel 13

This chapter continues the theme of prophecy. Here the LORD denounces both the false prophet and false prophetess.

The false prophets are compared to jackals and shoddy builders (vv. 1–16). The inspiration for their message is their own imaginations (vv. 2–3). God calls these messages 'false visions' and 'lying divinations' (vv. 6–9). The outcome of their words is that they mislead God's people, comforting the people with words of peace when the opposite is coming (vv. 10, 16). Like jackals they burrow among ruins to speed the decay of a city, instead of reinforcing the protective wall (v. 5). God's response to these builders who construct superficially attractive walls is that they will perish under the weight of the walls when they crumble; they will be excluded from God's people and excluded from the Promised Land (vv. 9, 14). Then they will recognise who God really is (vv. 9, 21, 23).

The false prophetesses are both similar to and different from their male counterparts (vv. 17–23). Again they prophesy out of their own imaginations, leading God's people astray. Yet the women are involved in magic, including charms, bands, veils, all of which are used to control, deceive and mislead their victims. Motivated by personal profit, they profane God's name by these evil practices (v. 19). The messages are in direct contrast to Ezekiel's ministry as a watchman (v. 22; cf. 3:16–21). God's response is that He will contend for His people, destroy the tools of the magic trade and save His people (vv. 20–21). In the end these sorceresses will also acknowledge who God is (vv. 21, 23).

Both the false prophet and false prophetess undermine the message that God had given Ezekiel.

REFLECTION

1. ***Beware! False prophets are still around today, motivated by financial gain and presenting messages their hearers want to hear (2 Tim. 4:3–4).***

2. ***Beware! If you present God's message, make sure you correctly handle the word of truth (2 Tim. 2:15).***

DAY 15

READ Ezekiel 14

Ezekiel's prophecies of God's judgement continue but again there is also hope.

First, God's judgement is against the secretly idolatrous elders and Israelites (vv. 1–11). Just like the elders who worshipped idols in secret in the temple vision (8:9–13), these elders and others in exile worship idols in their hearts (vv. 3–4). They come to seek a word from God via the prophet, but God answers rhetorically: 'Should I let them enquire of me at all?' Yet He still seeks to restore the relationship with His people (v. 4). To this end He urges them to repent, and this counsel is not just for the Israelites but also, somewhat surprisingly, for any others sojourning in Israel (vv. 6–7). But if there is no repentance, there will be excommunication and death, for false prophet and inquirer alike (vv. 8–9). Since both have turned away from God, He confirms them in their choice by enticing the prophet to utter a prophecy (v. 9). Nonetheless, the aim of God's judgement is to restore the covenant relationship (v. 11).

Second, God's judgement is against Jerusalem (vv. 12–23). Perhaps some of the exiles thought, 'If a righteous element could be found in the city, God might spare the city' (cf. Gen. 18). They held this hope especially since some probably had family there (vv. 16, 18, 20). Yet God responds several times to the effect that, 'Even if Noah, Job and Daniel were in the city, they would only save their own lives, not those of anyone else.' These three were known for their righteousness and obedience, in contrast to those around them. But even these heroes would not be able to save any others because of the utter depravity of Jerusalem. So God's classic 'disastrous acts of judgement' will descend upon the people (vv. 15–21). God's mercy prevails again, however: some survivors will come out to prove that God's judgement is fair and deserved. How will this be demonstrated? By seeing how wicked the saved are, people will know how righteous God's punishment is (vv. 22–23).

REFLECTION

At one time we were just as wicked as those in Jerusalem. But praise God! We are also survivors, not because of our righteousness, but because of His mercy shown to us in Christ Jesus (Tit. 3:3–7).

READ Ezekiel 15

Ezekiel 15 begins a series of three parables or extended metaphors.

This first parable sheds further light on why God's judgement came against Jerusalem. In the Old Testament Israel is often compared to a vine (e.g. Ps. 80:8–16; Jer. 2:21). This parable describes the uselessness of the wood of a vine (vv. 1–5), especially after it has been pruned (vv. 2–4). The wood of the vine is so soft it cannot even be used make pegs to hang things on (v. 3). When it has been used as firewood it is even more useless (v. 5). Once burned, it will go back into the fire again (v. 7; cf. 5:4). This parable illustrates Jerusalem's situation (vv. 6–8). God will judge those within Jerusalem because, like the wood of the vine, they are useless. All that is left for them is the fire of God's judgement (v. 6).

The reason for judgement is explained at the end of the chapter. As the LORD says through the prophet, it is because Jerusalem has 'been unfaithful' (v. 8). That is the people have turned away from God, especially by seeking after and trusting idols. Since they have done this, they are no longer different from the nations, and so they are useless. They no longer reflect God's character to the nations. Although the fire of God's judgement also has a purifying effect elsewhere in the Old Testament (e.g. Isa. 1:25; Mal. 3:2–3), it does not here. God's fire is only for destructive purposes. Historically the fire of God's judgement came by the hand of the Babylonians in 597 BC (with the 'first burning') then 586 BC (the 'second burning').

In short, Jerusalem is only fit for the fire of God's judgement – once and then again – because their faithlessness has made them useless.

REFLECTION

Israel's failure or worthlessness as a vine in the Old Testament looks forward to Jesus, the true vine and the true Israel (John 15:1). We are to abide in Him and bear fruit, or else we too are only fit for pruning and burning (John 15:4–6).

READ Ezekiel 16

This second extended metaphor is not for the faint of heart. It is lewd, deeply disturbing and as subtle as a sledgehammer. It is designed to shock the Israelite hearers, exposing their full-frontal depravity in order to break their entrenched spiritual adultery against God.

The image a reader cannot get away from as they read this chapter is 'whore' or 'prostitute' (mentioned twenty-one times in sixty-three verses). Jerusalem has been promiscuous, running off with all-comers – worshipping foreign idols and coupling with foreign nations (vv. 15–29). She even sacrificed her children (borne to God) in her foreign religious rituals (v. 20–21). Yet Jerusalem is worse than a normal sex worker because instead of accepting payment for her services, she actually pays her clients (vv. 30–34).

This is what God gets in return for His love and grace in rescuing her. She had been abandoned as a newborn, tossed aside to die (vv. 1–5), yet He nurtured her, raised her and married her when she became of age. He even adorned her with fine garments and jewellery, and she ascended to royalty (vv. 6–14). So much for gratitude.

Indeed, Jerusalem is depicted as behaving worse than Sodom and Samaria (vv. 44–52). Pride, gluttony, complacency and neglect in helping the poor are among her sins. Sodom and Samaria were wicked, but in contrast Jerusalem makes them look righteous! We know what happened to both Sodom and Samaria; we know what will happen to Jerusalem. The judgement on her will be just (v. 52); it will fit the crime and will even be carried out by her lovers (vv. 35–43).

Yet there is a twist. God will restore Jerusalem, and along with her also Samaria and Sodom (vv. 53–58). The central problem is that Jerusalem has broken the covenant with Him. Jerusalem has forgotten her covenant with God and forgotten His gracious rescue (vv. 22, 43). But there is hope because God remembers and is faithful to His covenant.

REFLECTION

We too have been rescued by God from our hopeless, ungodly state. May we always remember His gracious salvation in Jesus (Rom. 5:6–11).

The last of the series of three parables is about eagles and vines.

The parable begins with a magnificent eagle that snips off a fresh shoot of a cedar and carries it off to a foreign land (vv. 1–4). This first eagle then takes a native seedling and carefully nurtures it into a vine. This vine responds to the eagle as the bird intended (vv. 5–6). Then a second, less impressive eagle appears, triggering a reorientation of the vine: it now stretches towards this second eagle, although it lacked nothing from the first (vv. 7–8).

Ezekiel essentially asks: 'Will this vine flourish, now that it has switched allegiance to the second eagle?' Of course not! Now the vine is exposed, vulnerable to the destructive east wind from the desert. Also the vine has incurred the wrath of the first eagle, who has every right to uproot the vine and strip its leaves (vv. 9–10).

What is the meaning of this parable? The first eagle is Nebuchadnezzar, who attacked Jerusalem and deported King Jehoiachin and the elite (portrayed as the crown of the cedar) to Babylon in 597 BC (2 Kgs. 24:10–17). The Babylonian king appointed Zedekiah (depicted as the lowly vine) to the throne (2 Kgs. 24:18). But instead of grateful loyalty, he rebelled against Nebuchadnezzar, and sought help from the Pharaoh of Egypt, the second eagle (vv. 11–15). Of course Zedekiah will suffer for his breaking his oath (vv. 16–17, 19–21). His mistake was more than just treachery; he offended God Himself (v. 18). For when he swore his loyalty, it would have been sworn in the LORD's name (cf. 2 Chr. 36:13).

Finally we return to the cedar sprig of vv. 3–4. Now the function of the first magnificent eagle is given to God, as He Himself will take a shoot from the cedar and plant it on a high mountain (vv. 22–23). This points to a time when Jehoiachin and his line can look forward to a glorious future dynasty, a time when God will be universally acknowledged (vv. 23–24). This will certainly happen because, unlike King Jehoiachin, what God says, He will do (v. 24). He has the power to exalt and humble.

REFLECTION

God still uses evil worldly empires to fulfil His purposes (cf. Hab. 1). Praise God that He remains in sovereign control over all.

DAY 19

READ Ezekiel 18

This chapter is the first of a pair with the similar theme of personal responsibility.

It begins with an oft-repeated proverb of the time. The gist of it is: our fathers sinned but we are suffering for it (vv. 1–2; cf. Jer. 31:27–30). God strongly refutes this thinking; instead, He asserts the notion of personal responsibility (vv. 3–4; cf. 19–20). He illustrates His point with a three-generation case study (vv. 5–18):

1. The righteous patriarch, who is careful to live in harmony with God, will live (vv. 5–9).
2. By contrast the wicked son, who is the opposite of the patriarch in his actions, will be accountable for his sin (vv. 10–13).
3. The grandson of the patriarch will live, however, because he does not follow the path of his father (14–18).

God continues by saying that a person's past also does not determine their future (vv. 21–24). The wicked person can turn away from sin and live, his sins forgotten. The righteous person can turn to sin and die, his righteous deeds forgotten.

But Ezekiel's audience does not think this is fair (v. 25–29). What is God's response? He repeats the same conclusion as vv. 21–24. His point? You can't rest on your laurels. It's not just the way we start that is important, but the way we finish. God weighs each person's actions in the present.

Of course all generations of Israelites are culpable for the judgement that is about to come upon Jerusalem and Judah. But God urges each individual to take responsibility for their own sin, to repent, and to seek righteousness and justice (vv. 30–32). Indeed, He yearns for each person to repent and find life (vv. 23, 32).

REFLECTION

God is just in His judgement: each person will suffer consequences for their individual sin. Yet even today God still takes no pleasure in the death of the wicked; instead, His desire is for 'everyone to come to repentance' (2 Pet. 3:9).

The theme of personal responsibility carries through to the princes of Israel. What is striking about this chapter is that it is a lament, or funeral dirge (cf. 2:10). It is not a lament about what has happened but what will happen to two lions and a vine.

The first lion grows up to maturity, but is then hunted and taken away (vv. 1–4). The lioness refers to the tribe of Judah, and the lion is Jehoahaz, the son of Josiah, who was deported to Egypt because of the evil he committed (2 Kgs. 23:31–34). The second lion is taken to Babylon, so is probably either Jehoiachin or Zedekiah (vv. 5–9; 2 Kgs. 24:15; 25:7). This lion is described as tearing prey, devouring men, seizing widows and laying waste to cities. Both kings (represented by the first and second lions) are responsible for God's judgement that comes upon them.

The imagery in the lament then shifts from lions to a vine (vv. 10–14). At first the vine flourishes due to abundant water. The branches are strong, fit for a ruler's sceptre, an image linked to Judah and the Davidic dynasty (cf. Gen. 49:10). But the strength will not last, as this vine is destined to be ripped out of the ground and burnt (vv. 12, 14; cf. 15:5, 7). The fire will spread to consume its fruit, the whole house of Israel (cf. 5:4).

In short, God will judge the Davidic kings for their disobedience. As in the previous chapter, God's promises to earlier Davidic descendants does not guarantee blessing for each Davidic descendant (see 2 Sam. 7:1–17). Each king is personally responsible and will face God's judgement based on their actions, but their actions also have national consequences.

REFLECTION

The failure of the Davidic kings from the line of Judah makes us yearn for David's greatest descendant. Jesus Christ, 'the Lion of the tribe of Judah, the Root of David', will one day rule all nations as the king of kings (Rev. 5:5; 19:15–16).

DAY 21

READ Ezekiel 20:1–44

Most history is written from a particular perspective, and this passage is no different. In it we find Israel's history presented through the lens of idolatry.

The elders again seek a word from the LORD through Ezekiel (vv. 1–4). In response they are confronted with a record of their forefathers' abominations. Indeed, God asserts that they were idolatrous right from their origin (vv. 5–9). Even in Egypt, when He commanded Israel to get rid of their idols, they rebelled. The rebellion continued with the generation in the wilderness (vv. 10–17). This generation was given the Law so that they might live; sadly they rejected it and a generation died.

The following generation did not learn from the terrible example of their fathers (vv. 18–26). They continued the rejection of God's Law and God even wanted to disperse them among the nations before they entered the Promised Land. Since Israel disregarded the Law, it led to their defilement and death.

As we anticipate, nothing changes once Israel is in the Promised Land (vv. 27–29). Life continues with idolatry practised as usual. Then we fast-forward to the present (vv. 30–31). God addresses the current generation in exile and He declares that they are just the same. And God won't allow idolators to enquire of Him (v. 31; cf. v 3; 14:3).

Nonetheless, there is hope for Israel (vv. 32–44). Yes, Israel will face God's judgement again, just like in the wilderness. But after the purging judgement, a purified people will re-enter the Land.

Israel's history as presented by Ezekiel is one of sustained, unmitigated rebellion and idolatry. Repeatedly God wanted to put an end to Israel but each time He withholds His hand for the sake of His own reputation (vv. 8–9, 13–14, 22). Fortunately for Israel, God's concern for His name overpowers His wrath – for there was and remains nothing that people can do to merit God's grace (v. 44).

REFLECTION

Our personal history shows that we are just as unworthy of God's mercy as the Israelites (e.g. Rom. 3:23). It is thus a great comfort to know that, in the end, God acts for the sake of His glory, not because of who we are or what we do.

DAY 22

READ Ezekiel 20:45 – 21:32

This section contains a parable and some sign-acts, all to do with judgement.

In the parable Ezekiel sets his face against the southland to prophesy against the forests (20:45–48). The message is actually for the people in the southern kingdom of Judah, all of whom will be affected by the fire of God's judgement. Yet the people either do not understand or take his message lightly (20:49). The message is reinforced in the next section, this time declaring the sword will be used as the means of God's judgement (21:1–5). Ezekiel then performs a sign-act, grieving and groaning to enact the suffering because of the terrifying judgement (21:6–7).

A sword is then prepared for slaying (21:8–17). Again Ezekiel is to cry in anguish for the sword will strike God's people, both prince and people alike. God's judgement is indiscriminate, slashing to the right and left. Yet the slaying will come to an end when God's fury is satisfied (21:17).

Ezekiel is asked to perform another sign-act, revealing who will wield the sword (21:18–27). The prophet is to mark a forked road for the king of Babylon to take: either to Jerusalem or to Rabbah of the Ammonites. The king then uses pagan divination to determine which road to take, which ironically leads to the will of God. It is thus clear that behind the siege and destruction of Jerusalem at the hand of Nebuchadnezzar stands the judgement of God (21:24, 27). Part of the judgement will be that Zedekiah is stripped of his royalty (21:25–26).

God's judgement extends beyond Judah, however (21:28–32). Although Ammon was bypassed previously, it too will suffer for it is among the wicked (21:29; cf. 21:25). Finally Babylon, the sword itself, will return to the land where it was created. Here it will be judged with a furious annihilation (21:30–32).

REFLECTION

Shockingly God uses evil worldly powers to fulfil His purposes. Indeed, He uses wicked, lawless men to bring forgiveness and righteousness to humankind (Acts 2:23). Nonetheless, that does not mean those evil powers will escape His judgement (see Hab. 2:6–20).

DAY 23

READ Ezekiel 22

The main focus of Ezekiel up to now has been God's judgement because of the religious sins of Israel. The focus shifts in this chapter.

Ezekiel acts as the prosecutor, judging the people primarily for their sin of bloodshed (vv. 1–5). Both the princes of Israel and the people are involved in social sins – sins committed against one another. The first list of sins is aimed at the princes of Israel (vv. 6–8). The next list includes others also (vv. 9–12). The sins mentioned in these lists mainly reflect the Holiness Code (Lev. 18–20). The point is that there is a comprehensive breaking of God's laws. Again the sins derive from the same fundamental problem: forgetting God (cf. 16:22, 43; Deut, 4:9; 8:1–20).

Another list of sins is targeted at specific groups of people in Israel: prophets, priests, princes and the people of the land (vv. 23–29). These leaders failed in their responsibility to guide and protect the people; indeed, they abused their positions to exploit the defenceless – the poor, the needy and the sojourner.

Of course God will judge Israel for this catalogue of sins, with a particular emphasis on bloodshed (vv. 13–22). He will disperse Israel among the nations and will consume the people's uncleanness. God uses the image of a furnace, which is often the place for refining or purifying by God (e.g. Isa. 48:10; Mal. 3:2–3). This is not true in this case, though. Here, rather than producing pure silver or gold, all that is produced in the furnace is the dross, the unwanted by-products. That's how debased Israel has become.

Yet God does not rush headlong into judgement. He searches for a righteous one among them, who would plead on their behalf (v. 30; cf. 13:5), like Moses in the past (e.g. Ps. 106:19–23). But this time He cannot find anyone. Then the righteousness of God's judgement is repeated: the people are held accountable for their sin (vv. 3, 4, 31).

REFLECTION

Praise God for Jesus who saves us from God's judgement by shedding His own blood for us (Rom. 5:8–9). He is our sure defence against God's wrath; He justifies the guilty; He cleanses those who have blood on their hands.

This chapter forms a pair with chapter 16. Now Ezekiel cranks up the shock-o-meter a notch.

Although both chapters describe idolatry (e.g. vv. 36–42) and foreign alliances, the emphasis in this chapter is on the latter. Oholah (Samaria) and Oholibah (Jerusalem) are married to Yahweh (v. 4; cf. 16:8). Yet they are unfaithful to their husband; even in the honeymoon period they run off with Egypt (v. 3). This is followed by dalliances with Assyria, Babylon and then Egypt again.

These couplings symbolise the alliances between Israel or Judah and these nations throughout their histories. To be sure, politically these alliances are expedient. Israel feels she needs assistance against military threats. But God views these agreements as betrayal against Him, the one with whom they had entered an exclusive covenant relationship.

Indeed, God is disgusted (v. 18). To Him both the northern and southern cities are shameless: they play the whore; they openly flaunt their nakedness; they present their breasts to be fondled (vv. 3, 18–19, 21). One of their paramours is described as having genitals like donkeys and emissions like stallions (v. 20). This graphic sexual imagery is not for titillation. It is to shock and shame Ezekiel's audience into realising the nature and degree of their offence before God. This is how God views their adultery.

For these acts of infidelity we expect God's judgement, and it is pronounced (vv. 22–49). Jerusalem's 'lovers' will be the executors, with punishment including mutilation and death (vv. 22–27), and also nakedness and humiliation (vv. 28–30). Both cities will drink the bitter cup of God's judgement (vv. 31–35). This judgement will be a deterrent to other cities and towns, and will reveal, once again, who God is and what He is like (vv. 46–49).

REFLECTION

As Israel's husband, God is jilted, angry and disgusted at Israel's adultery. We, as the church, are in an exclusive covenant relationship with Christ. May we always seek to be faithful to Him and Him alone. And may we remain firmly devoted to our husband or wife, since this earthly relationship reflects that of Christ and the church (Eph. 5:22–33).

READ Ezekiel 24

Here we reach a turning point for Israel and for the prophet.

Finally, after years of prediction and warning, the Babylonian siege of Jerusalem begins (vv. 1-2). It is the beginning of the end for the city. The parable that follows makes it clear that Jerusalem will be no protection for its inhabitants (vv. 3–14). While it begins with a happy cooking song (vv. 3–5), the song then changes to a minor key (vv. 6–14). God then attacks Jerusalem, describing it as 'a city of bloodshed' (vv. 6, 9; cf. ch 22), full of corrosion. Human blood is spilled and even left out in the open (vv. 7–8; cf. Lev. 17:13). The corroded pot (v. 6) symbolises the city, rotten to the core. The 'meat' (v. 10) is Jerusalem, its people, who will be cremated without regard for their rank or importance. A bonfire is then made to cleanse the pot (v. 11). This is a terrifying picture of the annihilation of Jerusalem and its inhabitants. In His wrath, God's judgement comes – a judgement that is just, irreversible and chilling.

It is also a turning point for Ezekiel, both good and heartbreaking (vv. 15–27). It is good because a messenger tells him that his tongue will soon be loosened (vv. 25–27; cf. 3:26). The heartbreaking element is that his beloved wife will be taken away from him as a sign-act for the people (vv. 15–24). Yet although 'the delight of [his] eyes' dies (v. 16), the prophet is not allowed to mourn publicly. What is the meaning of this? It is that Jerusalem – the delight of the exiles' eyes – will be destroyed, but they are not to mourn as if it were an unexplained tragedy. Instead they are to groan to one another as they accept their guilt, and the fact that Jerusalem's destruction is God's just punishment for their sin.

REFLECTION

To be God's servant can be very costly. We only have to think of Christian martyrs and missionaries to see this. Yet we can trust in God's sovereign plan, the mysterious ways He uses us for His purposes of salvation. Perhaps Ezekiel's wife's death might have led some to repent. Ezekiel's suffering in a sense shared and anticipated the suffering of God, who gave up His own Son – the ultimate turning point in history – so that many more might be saved.

DAY 26

READ Ezekiel 25

As the Babylonian army bears down on Jerusalem, the focus shifts from judgement against Israel to judgement against its surrounding nations (Ezek. 25–32). The structure of these prophetic oracles against the nations is like a seesaw.[2] Oracles against six nations (25:1 – 28:23, a total of ninety-seven verses) are balanced by oracles against Egypt (29:1 – 32:32, also a total of ninety-seven verses). The fulcrum that balances these two sets of oracles is a message for Israel (28:24–26).

In relation to the land of Israel, these nations are addressed in clockwise order. Ammon to the east is first (25:1–7), followed by Moab (vv. 8–11), Edom to the south (vv. 12–14) and Philistia to the west (vv. 15–17). The oracles have the same general structure:

- A reason for the judgement.
- A judgement outlined (introduced by 'therefore ...').
- The outcome – God is recognised for who He is ('Then they/you will know that I am the LORD').

The reason for God's judgement against Ammon and Moab is similar. Both of these nations laughed and gloated when Jerusalem was attacked and the people taken away (vv. 3, 6, 8). Edom and Philistine were also similar in their motivation: revenge against Israel (vv. 12, 15). These old adversaries of Israel wanted to get even, so they grabbed their chance to act maliciously against God's people.

But Israel will have the last laugh because God will pay back these nations for their actions. God will punish these nations, bringing destruction to them, including by the hand of nomads from the Arabian desert (vv. 4, 10; cf. Jer. 49:28).

The outcome is that God will be universally recognised for who He is. In His acts of judgement He will be seen as the one and only true and living God. He is the king over not just Israel but over all nations on earth.

REFLECTION

Today God is not recognised by all as the King of the universe. But a day will come when all nations will face God's judgement. Then everyone will recognise His sovereignty and that of His Son (Rom. 14:10–11; Phil. 2:10–11).

Two foreign nations are singled out by Ezekiel: Egypt (29:1 – 32:32) and Tyre (26:1 – 28:19). These two nations were particularly staunch in their resistance against Babylon. Tyre was a city-state built mainly on a rocky island on the Mediterranean coast. Its location and harbours not only allowed the Phoenician city to rise to become a trading powerhouse but also provided natural protection from military invaders. Yet this offered no protection against God.

Ezekiel's oracle against Tyre follows the same pattern we saw in the last chapter. First, the reason for God's judgement is outlined: Tyre rubbed her hands with glee at the fall of Jerusalem, for it opened the door for Tyre to gain sole control of trade in the region (v. 2).

Second, this exploitation is judged by God (vv. 3–14). Nations, including Babylon, will attack Tyre. Its destruction will include the island as well as the mainland (v. 6). Tyre's wealth will be plundered; this is poetic justice considering the city's opportunism (v. 12; cf. v. 2). This prophecy will be fulfilled in stages. The city will negotiate a settlement with Nebuchadnezzar, who will exert political control over it (c. 572 BC). But the city's complete destruction will not come until the time of Alexander the Great (332 BC). Then Tyre will be completely destroyed (v. 14).

Third, the outcome of Tyre's downfall is that it will have a ripple effect on surrounding coastlands (vv. 15–18). The nearby princes will respond with a mixture of grief and fear. They will mourn the fall of such a great empire but also the economic implications of Tyre's collapse. Also described in the princes' lament is a description of the terror imposed by Tyre in its prime (v. 17). The final verses make it clear that it is the LORD who is behind the destruction (vv. 19–21).

REFLECTION

In our age, with the presence of many economic powerhouses, not just nations but also companies, it is sobering to be reminded that these powerhouses are being watched. God may judge their exploitation too. With the recent global financial crises we know that these economic empires are not invulnerable.

DAY 28

READ Ezekiel 27

This chapter is a lamentation for Tyre. The city is portrayed as a grand, self-assured trading ship, built of local and imported materials (vv. 3–7). The crew of the ship are drawn from Phoenician cities and include mercenary soldiers from foreign lands (vv. 8–11). Next the city's trading partners and the commodities traded are detailed (vv. 12–25). There is a huge spread of trading partners, from Tarshish (possibly Spain) to Arabia and Mesopotamia. Among the list of commodities are many luxurious items.

Suddenly the ship is destroyed (vv. 26–27). An east wind blows up, wrecking the ship, along with all its crew. The ship and the city's wealth sink without a trace. People on the land and in other ships are aghast at what they witness (vv. 28–31). They mourn bitterly with genuine grief at the downfall of their trading partner. Why do they respond so? As is made clear in the following lamentation (vv. 32–36; cf. the larger lamentation), it is because Tyre's prosperity meant the prosperity of its trading partners. Similarly today nations hope that important global economies, such as China or the United States, will continue to grow economically, for this means the rest of the world, particularly its trading partners, will also benefit. Tyre's economy was just as crucial for the region. 'Who is like Tyre?' the people in effect lament (v. 32), for the city was matchless.

Yet all Tyre's wealth, economic power and international standing was gained without a nod towards God. 'I am perfect in beauty' the city arrogantly asserts, not 'God has made me perfect in beauty.' It is all 'self-made' wealth, based on hard work, extensive trading networks and greed. So God brings an east wind to obliterate such self-importance.

REFLECTION

Tyre's attitude and attainments are repeated throughout history, right down to today. Achievement of worldly success and acclaim without acknowledging God continues unabated. As Christians do we look up to these ideals? Are we tempted to follow the path of Tyre? We need to be mindful of what God's response will be. Also remember what Jesus says: we cannot serve both God and money (Matt. 6:24).

DAY 29

READ Ezekiel 28

Next the focus is on the pride of the leader of Tyre (vv. 1–19), followed by an oracle against Sidon (vv. 20–23) and then a succinct word about the effect of the judgement against the nations on Israel (vv. 24–26).

The king of Tyre, King Ethbaal II, claims divine status and authority, or at least acts as if he is divine (vv. 1–10). The self-made wealth of his city is coupled with massive arrogance. Yet God will put the king in his place. His fate will be the same as Jerusalem, as he is cut down to size by foreigners. Indeed, this 'god' will be slain by the hands of vile and unclean people. Then follows a lamentation using imagery from the creation of humankind and Eden, vividly illustrating the heights from which Ethbaal has fallen (vv. 11–19). Just as the first humans were vice-regents under God with dominion over all creation, so Ethbaal enjoyed the God-granted status of king. Ethbaal is even described as 'a guardian cherub' (v. 14), but this greatness only underlines his fall. The sins outlined lead to God's judgement of the king, which is similar to the Fall in the Garden of Eden – expulsion and death.

Next is a brief oracle against Tyre's neighbour, Sidon (vv. 20–23). There is no clear charge against the city; perhaps it was involved in the revolt against Babylon during Zedekiah's reign (Jer. 27:3) and perhaps its offences included derision against Judah (cf. 25:1 – 26:6). In any case God's glory will be manifested through His judgement and they will recognise who the LORD is.

The effect of the oracles against foreign nations on Israel forms the fulcrum for the whole section (chapters 25–32). The significance for the Israelites is that judgement on the nations means peace and security for Israel in their land, once their enemies have been wiped out (vv. 24–26).

REFLECTION

The pride of the king of Tyre finds echoes throughout the Bible. Pride was a foremost characteristic of the builders of the Tower of Babel (Gen. 11:1–9), and Tyre will also be a paradigm for Herod's arrogance and fall. The description of 'Babylon' in Revelation 17–18 also draws on the fall of Tyre. Today God's opposition to pride continues (1 Pet. 5:5).

DAY 30

READ Ezekiel 29

The second major section of the oracles against the nations concerns Egypt (Ezek. 29–32). Why is so much space devoted to Egypt? At the time the prophecy is dated, Jerusalem had been under siege for about a year. Perhaps some hoped that Hophra, King of Egypt, would help out Israel. But Ezekiel (and his contemporary Jeremiah; see Jer. 37:5–8; 44:30) viewed Nebuchadnezzar as the LORD's servant. Hence those who resisted the Babylonian king resisted the LORD Himself.

There are two dominant pictures of Egypt (vv. 1–16):

1. As a great sea monster combined with a crocodile. The king of Egypt was boasting that he created and owns the Nile River (v. 3; cf. v. 9). In effect he claimed to be the source of the land's fertility; of course this is blasphemous. So this sea monster will be dragged out of the stream and cast into the desert to rot.
2. As a reed (v. 6). But Egypt is not useful as a staff or a crutch; that is Egypt is not reliable as an ally of Israel. So Pharaoh will be defeated and the reign of Egypt as a world power will come to an end. Yet there is hope that Egypt will be restored (vv. 13–16; cf. Isa. 19:19–25).

The next prophecy (vv. 17–21) is the last recorded prophecy of Ezekiel, dated sixteen years after the siege of Jerusalem. There is an adjustment of Ezekiel's previous prophecy (26:14). Tyre is reduced to vassal status but is not razed to the ground, neither did Babylon receive a great reward. So God grants Egypt to Babylon instead of Tyre. As mentioned previously, a successful siege did take place, under Alexander. So the prophecy is eventually fulfilled.

The focus of prophecy is not the precise outline of future events but the proclamation of God's purpose. Also, often with prophecy we can see multiple fulfilments.

REFLECTION

Although prophecy might not be fulfilled in ways we expect, we can trust that God is sovereign and will bring His word to pass. As Christians we can see how Old Testament prophecies often have an immediate fulfilment, followed by another fulfilment in Christ, and often a final fulfilment when Christ returns (cf. 2 Cor. 1:20).

DAY 31

The next oracle against Egypt (vv. 1–19) is not dated, but was probably proclaimed around the time of the siege of Jerusalem (cf. vv. 20–26). At this time there was a hope that Egypt could rescue Israel from the Babylonian army. This chapter makes it clear that the hope would be in vain.

This is because the 'day of the LORD' (v. 3) is upon Egypt. This momentous day finds echoes with other parts of the Old Testament (especially the Prophets), pointing to a time of God's salvation and judgement. That second element is prominent here as judgement will come upon:

1. Egypt, as it will suffer the sword, along with other nations (vv. 2–5).
2. Egypt's allies. In their pride they will be brought low (vv. 6–9).
3. Egypt's army, who will suffer devastation by the hand of Nebuchadnezzar (vv. 10–12).
4. Egypt's idols, strongholds and cities, which will be destroyed (vv. 13–18).

Again the outcome of these judgements will be that people will recognise who God really is (v. 19).

In the next section Ezekiel drives home the point of Israel's vain hope in Egypt as a rescuer (vv. 20–26). This oracle is dated near the time when Hophra, the King of Egypt, marched against Babylon, leading to a temporary reprieve for Jerusalem (Jer. 37:7–8). God says He will break not just the strong arm of Pharaoh, used to wield the sword in battle, but also his weak arm. Egypt will be completely debilitated in battle. By contrast God will strengthen the arm of Babylon. The outcome is a foregone conclusion: Egypt will be mortally wounded, its inhabitants dispersed among the nations – the same judgement Israel will face. It is clear that Babylon is the means that God will bring judgement, not just on Israel but also on Egypt. Since there is no hope for Egypt, there is no hope for Jerusalem against Babylon.

REFLECTION

The absolute sovereignty of God is reasserted once again. No one can stand against Him; He pulls the strings of all history. We look forward to another 'day of the Lord' when Jesus returns, which will also be marked by judgement and salvation (e.g. 2 Pet. 3:10).

DAY 32

READ Ezekiel 31

This new oracle against Egypt is dated two months after the previous one. In it Egypt is compared to Assyria in its greatness but the same fate befalls both these empires.

Assyria is pictured as a magnificent cedar (vv. 3–9). This tree symbolises majesty, with its wood often used to build temples and palaces. Drawing on the ancient near-Eastern myth of the 'cosmic tree', connecting the world with the netherworld and the heavens, Assyria is depicted as dominating all the neighbouring empires (v. 6). The splendour of the cedar is such that even the trees in the Garden of Eden envy it (vv. 8–9).

It is such greatness that sets up Assyria for a catastrophic fall (vv. 10–14). Indeed, Assyria, and also Egypt, becomes proud because of its lofty standing and strength. But as the saying goes, 'Pride comes before a fall' (cf. Prov. 16:18). Assyria fell to Babylon about twenty-five years before the time of Ezekiel, so the defeat would still be fresh in the minds of Ezekiel's hearers. The cedar of Assyria was cut down; the same fate would befall Egypt at the hands of the Babylonians. Those who flourished under its shadow would be dispersed (v. 12).

God's judgement on Egypt also includes sending it down to Sheol (vv. 15–18). God's control is underlined by the fivefold repetition of 'I' in verses 15–16. Similar to the oracle against Tyre, the downfall of an influential empire will have widespread reverberations – the nations will shake when they hear the resounding thud of the fall.

REFLECTION

Assyria and Egypt became arrogant because of their lofty positions. They thought that their achievements were won simply through the sweat of their brow and the strength of their hands. But God corrects this thinking in verse 9: 'I made [the cedar] beautiful.' God is behind the magnificence of nations. We would do well to remember that He is also behind all we have, do and achieve. As Paul says, 'In [God] we live and move and have our being' (Acts 17:28).

READ Ezekiel 32

The final two oracles against Egypt describe its destruction and descent (vv. 1–16; 17–32). They are both dated to after the fall of Jerusalem.

The first oracle begins with how Egypt sees itself: as a lion among the nations (v. 2). But the reality is that it is like a sea monster, an adversary of God. The creature is caught in a net by God, along with a whole throng, then hurled into an open field (vv. 3–4; cf. 29:5). The cosmic picture language underlines the cataclysmic effects of the destruction of Egypt on other nations (vv. 5–10). Babylon will be the instrument of God's judgement (vv. 11–16).

The second oracle is a dirge over Egypt (vv. 17–32). The self-exalting nation is sent down to the underworld, the realm of the dead. Seven nations are mentioned as inhabitants of the underworld, including Assyria (vv. 22–30). These nations had spread terror while in the land of the living (vv. 23–26, 30, 32), but will now bear their shame in the place of the dead (vv. 24–25, 30). Along with these nations, Egypt will now share the shame of the uncircumcised, unburied and those slain by the sword (cf. 31:18). Egypt is not alone in the pit, bringing some cold comfort – her fate is the same as the other nations (v. 31).

It is disturbing that God strikes terror in the land of the living (v. 32). Sheol is depicted as the realm of the dead in the Old Testament, but a clearer picture is revealed in the New Testament. When Christ returns again, there will be a final judgement, after which those who do not recognise Jesus as King will be cast into hell, a place of eternal punishment. This is a truly terrifying place, one that must be avoided at all costs (e.g. Mark 9:42–48).

REFLECTION

Praise God for Jesus, who took the punishment for sin that we deserved, saving us from hell (e.g. 2 Cor. 5:21). Instead, we look forward to eternal life in a new heaven and new earth (Rev. 21:1).

The oracles against the nations are now complete (chapters 25–32) and attention turns back to the house of Israel. This is the second half of the turning point of the book (cf. chapter 24). Jerusalem finally falls in this chapter, but before it does Ezekiel reminds his hearers of two responsibilities.

The first responsibility belongs to the prophet himself (vv. 1–9). He must continue to act as a watchman, warning the people of God's judgement (cf. 3:16–21). Ezekiel must continue with this task, even after the destruction of Jerusalem. The second responsibility belongs to the people (vv. 10–20). In response to their cry of despair Ezekiel reiterates the mercy of God: He wants all people to turn to Him and live. The message of the importance of individual responsibility for sin is repeated (cf. chapter 18).

Then it is announced: 'The city has fallen!' (v. 21). Ezekiel is vindicated because what he's been prophesying happens. His tongue is loosened (v. 22), just as predicted (24:27; cf. 3:26). Now that he's proven to be a genuine prophet, surely people will pay attention to him. Or will they?

Ezekiel then proclaims a message about the survivors in Jerusalem (vv. 23–29). They will continue the Abrahamic promise, but the prophet proclaims that the future lies with the exiles. Indeed, since the survivors act wickedly, they too will suffer God's judgement (vv. 25–29). Finally, God reports to Ezekiel the people's response to his messages (vv. 30–33). The people come to be entertained by his words, but sadly they don't take them to heart. As God warned the prophet, the people have stubborn hearts so they won't take His word seriously (e.g. 3:7).

REFLECTION

External identity does not save the people of Israel. Being a member of God's people is not inherited. What is required is a response of faith, an internal commitment to God, a heartfelt obedience. This is the same message as in the New Testament: through faith in Christ we are all children of God, irrespective of ethnicity (e.g. Gal. 3:23–29).

The shepherd was a common metaphor for leaders and kings in the ancient near East (cf. 2 Sam. 5:2; 7:7–8). Here the Israelite shepherds are derided for being wicked, careless and self-serving, and for shirking their responsibility (vv. 1–10). Instead of looking after the flock, they were serving themselves at the expense of the lives of the sheep. The sheep are scattered and become prey for wild animals.

But this is no ordinary flock; this is God's flock ('my sheep' is used in v. 6 and 'my flock' occurs five times in vv. 6–10). The kings were meant to lead God's people. So God is 'against' them (v. 10; cf. 5:8), a phrase usually reserved for His enemies. And He will rescue His sheep from the evil shepherds.

God Himself takes over. As a good shepherd, He will gather in, tend and feed His sheep (vv. 11–16). In other words, He will be the complete opposite to Israel's shepherds. God's initiative and sovereign action is emphasised by the repetition of 'I will' (which appears eleven times in vv. 11–16). Also, He will lead them justly – not only will the shepherds be judged, but so too will the sheep (vv. 17–22). The bad sheep in these verses probably refers to those exploiting others within the exilic community.

After God has saved His flock, they can look forward to a time of true peace and of lush pastures in the land (vv. 23–31). God's people can look forward to a Davidic ruler (vv. 23–24), perfect shalom (vv. 25–29) and the full restoration of the covenant relationship (vv. 25, 30–31).

REFLECTION

This chapter anticipates Jesus, who is 'the good shepherd' (John 10:11–18). By making this statement, Jesus was claiming to be the true king, the LORD in the flesh. He would seek and save the lost sheep of Israel (Matt. 10:6; cf. Luke 15:3–7); He will separate the sheep from the goats (Matt. 25:31–46; cf. Ezek. 34:17). Today those who are pastors in the church are shepherds under the chief Shepherd. They should exercise leadership not for personal gain but to serve as godly role models for God's flock (1 Pet. 5:1–5).

DAY 36

READ Ezekiel 35:1 – 36:15

In today's passage an oracle against a mountain in Edom is followed by a message of restoration of the mountains of Israel.

Mt Seir is representative of Edom, just as Mt Zion is of Israel (cf. Deut. 2:1–4). Edom was an arch-enemy of Israel throughout its history. There had been constant hostility between the Edomites (Esau's descendants) and Israel (35:5; cf. Num. 20:14–21). In more recent history the Edomites are accused on three counts of:

1. Hostility (35:5; cf. Obad. 8–14).
2. Expansion into Israel (35:10). Edom has no right to possess the land; it belongs to God (Lev. 25:23).
3. Boasting and gloating over the destruction of Jerusalem (35:12–15).

Thus Edom has to be dealt with before Israel can enjoy long-lasting peace. Because of their crimes, God will judge Edom, with the punishment fitting the crime (35:14–15).

Previously the mountains of Israel were judged (6:2); now they will be restored. The land had become the object of peoples' malicious talk and slander because it did not provide security and prosperity for its inhabitants (36:3, 6). Instead it was known as a devourer of its people (36:13–15). God reiterates His response to the crimes of Edom and the nations – they will bear their own scorn (36:7). Yet Israel and their land's humiliation will be reversed (36:8–12). Israel will return to populate the land, with the abundance of life reminiscent of the blessing at creation (Gen. 1:22, 28). Indeed, God will bless them even more than before (36:11).

REFLECTION

Part of the trauma for the exiles would have been that they thought God had abandoned His covenant promises to them, including the promise of land (e.g. Gen. 12:7; 15:7). So this prophecy would have been a great comfort for them. God kept His promise: some did return to the land in the post-exilic period. But the complete fulfilment of the grand blessings promised in this passage await Jesus' return. As Christians we look forward to our heavenly inheritance (see 1 Pet. 1:3–5; cf. Eph. 1:11–14).

DAY 37

READ Ezekiel 36:16–38

This key passage highlights God's restoration of Israel, although His motivation for doing so is not what we might expect.

Since Israel profaned the land by its sins, God removed the nation from the land. Yet wherever they went they profaned God's name because people were left to conclude that either Yahweh had abandoned His people or that He was not as powerful as other gods (vv. 16–21). In ancient near-Eastern thinking, the defeat of Israel signalled the defeat of the LORD; He was seen as a loser!

So God is now roused to defend His character and reputation among the nations (vv. 22–24). Made to look ordinary or common, He will act to restore His holiness and sovereignty. This is His motivation for restoring Israel. He does not operate primarily out of compassion or love, or because He feels sorry for Israel. Here God acts to restore His holy name among the nations. A just God has to punish His people, even though it causes His name to be profaned, but then He acts again to restore His people, yes, but ultimately to restore His name.

God will also transform His people's relationship with Him (vv. 25–32). They will receive a wholesale cleansing from sin; a new, responsive heart and His Spirit, allowing His people to obey Him. He will renew His covenant with them (v. 28). Israel will then remember its past sins, and this will lead to self-loathing (vv. 31–32; cf. 6:9).

Then finally Israel will enjoy abundant blessing in the land (vv. 33–38; cf. vv. 9–12). When God completes His salvation and restoration, the surrounding nations will acknowledge His special relationship with His people and His land. His name will be vindicated.

REFLECTION

God truly is sovereign over the whole earth; He alone deserves all glory and honour (1 Tim. 1:17). He acts in history so that His people and the nations may know that He is God. The picture of an Eden-like paradise where God will dwell among His people will be fulfilled in the 'new heaven and ... new earth' (Rev. 21:1–3). Here too we will find multitudes of people worshipping Him for who He is (Rev. 7:9–10).

READ Ezekiel 37

The first part of today's chapter contains one of Ezekiel's best-known prophecies (vv. 1–14). The second part contains another sign-act about Israel's future reunification (vv. 15–28).

The prophecy opens with a ghastly scene: thousands upon thousands of dry bones scattered over a valley floor. God asks the prophet to wander among the bones, and then He asks a strange question: 'Can these bones live?' (v. 3). Ezekiel knows God can do it, but does He want to? Ezekiel doesn't have to wonder very long because God asks him to prophecy the word of the LORD. Then, miraculously, tendons and flesh appear over the bones to form a cadaver. But there's no life in them until God breathes His breath, His spirit, into the bones (vv. 1–10).

Thus this resurrection takes two steps: first, the formation of a lifeless corpse; second, the infusion of breath to make a living being. The same two steps happened in the creation of the Adam. In other words, God needs to exert His creative powers again. The exiles feel like the bleached bones; their hopes have died. Yet God will resurrect Israel; His Spirit will breathe new life; He will bring His people back into the Promised Land (vv. 11–14).

The sign-act illustrates how Israel will be one nation again (vv. 15–28). The joining together of the two sticks represents the southern (Judah) and northern (Ephraim) kingdoms reunified. Currently splintered and dispersed among the nations, they will be united under one Davidic king and one covenant, worshipping one God in one sanctuary (vv. 24–28). Again God's initiative is emphasised ('I am' occurs once and 'I will' six times in vv. 19–23).

There will also be an internal overhaul of God's people (vv. 23–24, 28; cf. 36:25–27). They will be God's cleansed, holy people, now obedient to God's laws. The covenant blessings will flow because it will be a new, eternal covenant (vv. 26–28).

REFLECTION

Thank God that we are cleansed, Spirit-filled and with a new heart that can obey God. The same Spirit that raised Jesus from the dead has breathed life into us (Rom. 8:11). God's powerful word (the gospel of Jesus) has brought us back from the dead. We are to live according to the Spirit (Rom. 8:4–5) and to put to death the misdeeds of the body (Rom. 8:13).

Within the flow of the book of Ezekiel, chapters 38–39 appear out of place. Chapters 33–48 generally concern the restoration of Israel. Yet chapters 38–39 are reminiscent of the oracles against the nations that we find in chapters 25–32. So how do they fit in their current location?

Chapters 38–39 concern the defeat and disposal of Gog from the land of Magog. The exact identification of this enemy is not clear, but the prophecy is set in the future, since Gog and his allies arm themselves for an assault against God's people, who have settled back in the land (vv. 1–9). From the start it is clear that God is controlling this conflict as He draws these seven allies out, each from the corners of the then-known world (v. 4; cf. v. 16). These hordes will want to plunder Israel for their wealth, now that God's people dwell securely under His blessing (vv. 10–13).

In response God will rise up to protect His people (vv. 14–23). Gog will become an object lesson for the surrounding nations, as they recognise His power and His commitment to His people (vv. 14–16). God's anger and jealousy are aroused again, this time against Israel's enemies (vv. 18–19). His judgement against the allies is described in cosmic and universal terms; this is not a normal battle (vv. 19–22). The typical divine judgements mostly experienced by Israel are now turned against the enemy. Finally the LORD's greatness will be manifest among the nations by His protection of Israel (v. 23).

Following chapters 38–39 God will return to His temple. So these chapters set the stage for His dwelling in His sanctuary by securing true peace and safety for His people in the land.

REFLECTION

The New Testament interpretation of Gog of Magog in Revelation follows a similar movement. Gog and Magog concerns the final battle between God and His enemies, occurring just before the final vision of the heavenly Jerusalem (Rev. 20–21). Throughout history God's enemies will threaten His people but the assurance is that God will win and His people will rest in security.

DAY 40

READ Ezekiel 39

This chapter repeats themes of the previous chapter, but emphasises Gog's slaughter and disposal. All that will happen to Gog will serve to reveal who the LORD is.

There is certainty that Gog will be defeated – God Himself will see to it (vv. 1–8). Previously God's name was profaned through the judgement of Israel (36:22–23) but the LORD will prevent this from happening again by defending His people (vv. 7–8). After Gog's defeat, Israel is called to join in the mop-up operation (vv. 9–16). Israel will collect the enemy's weapons and use them as firewood. There will be enough to kindle fires for seven years! Israel will also be involved in the burial of their vanquished enemies, in order to cleanse the land.

What happens next is ghastly (vv. 17–20). Birds and beasts are invited to join in a sacrificial feast, including unclean animals. They will eat the slain enemy, those who haven't been buried yet. Many taboos are broken in this scene: drinking blood, eating human flesh, and the presence of unclean animals. This is a repulsive scene, especially for Ezekiel, one with a priestly background. Nonetheless, the scene underlines the complete destruction of those who oppose God (cf. Rev. 19:17–21).

The outcome will be that God's sovereignty in history will be displayed before the nations (vv. 21–29) – not only in the defeat of Gog, but also in the way He treats His own people. First, He sends them into exile as judgement for their sin (vv. 22–24). Second, He restores His people (vv. 25–27). Then they will know that He is the LORD (v. 28). This judgement on His people won't happen again, since God will give them His Spirit (v. 29).

Ultimately God will be acknowledged and glorified for who He is. He is holy; He is all-powerful; He is the judge of all. Previously God said He would not spare Israel, nor would He have pity regarding Israel's judgement (e.g. 5:11; 7:4). Now He is also shown to be merciful and compassionate (v. 25).

REFLECTION

Praise God that we have also been sealed with the Spirit (Eph. 1:13; 4:30). We have security in knowing that the Spirit is the guarantee of our inheritance.

We may find the first few chapters of Ezekiel's final vision (chapters 40–48) a little mind-numbing. Yet we can learn about God's holiness even in the plan of the temple.

It was the twenty-fifth year of the exile (v. 1). Twenty-five years is half a jubilee, and the beginning of the year also signified a special time of hope of liberation. The number twenty-five is emphasised in the rest of the chapter also in the measurements (vv. 13, 21, 25, 29, 30, 33, 36). This square number and the square measurements in the temple point to symmetry, an idealised geometry. The ideal nature of the vision is also underscored by the description of the city of Jerusalem atop a 'very high mountain' (v. 2).

Ezekiel's supernatural guide begins the tour at the outer wall. The wall is thick as well as high. On each of the east, north and south sides the walls have massive gates with gatehouses (vv. 6–16, 20–23, 24–27). The wall and gates separate the holy (within the temple area) from the common (cf. 42:20).

Within the temple compound there are also graded areas of holiness. Just inside the outer wall is the outer court (vv. 17–19). Its increased holiness is indicated by it being seven steps higher than the ground outside (vv. 22, 26). The breadth of the outer court (50m; v. 19) provides a buffer zone around the holier area of the inner court and temple.

The inner court is yet another step up in holiness. Three gates allow access into the inner court (vv. 28–37), and at each gate it takes eight steps up to reach it from the outer court (vv. 31, 34, 38). There are rooms and facilities for priests to wash and slaughter sacrifices (vv. 38–47). There are also chambers for Zadokites, those exclusively involved in serving God (vv. 44–47). Reaching the vestibule of the temple requires ascending another ten steps (v. 49).

REFLECTION

The design of the temple compound portrayed the idea of increased holiness and restricted access the closer one moved to the temple itself at the centre. Through Christ we now have unrestricted access to God, so let us draw near to Him 'with a sincere heart in full assurance of faith' (Heb. 10:19–22).

DAY 42

READ Ezekiel 41

Today we find descriptions and measurements of the temple itself. It would have been the exciting climax for at least one person.

Ezekiel's vision continues with a description of the temple building (vv. 1–4, 13–15). It is detailed with precise measurements. Like Moses' tabernacle and Solomon's temple, the building is divided into two main rooms: the outer sanctuary and the Most Holy Place. An increasing holiness is represented by the decreasing size of the entrances: 7m (main entrance; 40:48) to 5m (larger sanctuary; 41:2) to 3m (entrance to Most Holy Place; 41:3).

The temple building is panelled with wood and decorated with palm trees and cherubim (vv. 16–20). Once again there are similarities with Solomon's temple, but it is simpler in decoration. The only furniture in the outer sanctuary is a wooden altar (v. 22) for the Zadokite priests to minister before God (44:16).

Around the temple building are ninety rooms, thirty on each level (vv. 5–12). Behind the temple to the west are a restricted area and a building (vv. 10, 12). Perhaps this is to protect from a rear approach to the temple.

The highlight is when the guide shows Ezekiel the Most Holy Place. The prophet doesn't actually enter it (v. 4). Nonetheless, can you imagine how exciting it would have been for Ezekiel? He had been groomed all his life to be a priest, then whisked away to Babylon before he began his ministry. Without a temple he couldn't function as a priest, and indeed he was called to be a prophet. But here he gets to peek inside the Most Holy Place, the place where only the high priest could enter. But someone is missing here. God is not present ... yet.

REFLECTION

The temple is holiness embodied in a physical structure. Amazingly holiness would be embodied in a person. No one has ever seen God, but Jesus Christ has made Him known in all His glory, all His splendour and all His holiness (John 1:14–18). Jesus says, 'The one who has seen me has seen the Father' (John 14:9).

In today's chapter Ezekiel returns to where he began the tour to consider the function of the temple complex (vv. 15–20). But before that he views the priest's chambers (vv. 1–14).

As Ezekiel leaves the temple building he is shown the chambers. These three-level buildings are on the north and south of the inner court complex. They function as a boundary area, reserved for activities that need to be contained for the sake of holiness. Holy offerings are to be placed and consumed in the rooms (v. 13). Eating offerings met the physical needs of the priests because they owned no land to produce crops (44:28–30). Priests are to leave their sacred clothes in these rooms so that they do not bring the holy items into contact with the profane in the outer court (v. 14).

Ezekiel then returns to the eastern gate of the outer wall, where he began the tour (vv. 15–20; cf. 40:6). The overall dimensions of the temple are a perfect square (250m x 250m). The ideal length and shape hints at a greater level of holiness than the tabernacle, in which only the Most Holy Place was square-shaped. The overall size of the temple compound is also much larger than Solomon's temple.

It is unlikely that the temple was meant to be rebuilt according to the description in Ezekiel 40–42. Indeed, those who returned to the land after the exile didn't build according to Ezekiel's vision. Nonetheless, since the temple was central to Israelite identity, it would have been a great comfort and encouragement for them to know that God would still be with them and that He would safeguard holiness in the future.

REFLECTION

The temple foreshadows Jesus, who is God's temple in a person (John 2:18–22). Jesus gives us the Holy Spirit, so that we are temples individually and as a church (e.g. 1 Cor. 6:19–20; Eph. 2:19–22). Praise God for His presence dwelling in each of us! And we live with the hope of a square-shaped heavenly Jerusalem (Rev. 21:16), where there will be no need for a temple because God and the Lamb will dwell with us directly (Rev. 21:22).

DAY 44

READ Ezekiel 43

Yahweh's return to the temple is the highlight of chapters 43–46. For God's people it was both a message of assurance and a word of challenge.

In the first part of this chapter (vv. 1–12) God's glory returns. The departure was slow and halting (Ezek. 10), but the return is rapid and direct (vv. 1–5). The glory of God fills not only the temple (e.g. 1 Kgs. 8:10–11) but also the whole earth (v. 2). Ezekiel's response is the same as before: worship (v. 3). Then God makes a momentous announcement of assurance: as the King, He will live with His people forever with the temple as His royal palace (vv. 7–9). But the divine King's presence requires a change in behaviour in the:

- Worship of dead kings (vv. 7, 9).
- Kings' encroachment into sacred space (v. 8).
- Detestable practices (v. 8).

The challenge for the people is to remove these abuses of the past.

Ezekiel is then to describe the temple to the people (vv. 10–11). Grasping the perfect proportions of the temple and especially the restriction of access will lead the people to feel ashamed of their past actions. This shame will then allow the people to follow the path of the prophet. In such humility the people will recognise that restoration was by God's grace alone. This instruction of the temple (v. 12) then continues into the next section.

The second part of the chapter describes God's provision for maintaining holiness (vv. 13–27). The altar is central to this (vv. 13–17). Before it is to be used, it must be purified and Israel's past sins cleansed (vv. 18–27). The burnt offerings are to be wholly given to God while the fellowship/peace offerings will have a communal element. Once more the wonderful assurance for God's people is that they will be acceptable to Him again (v. 27). God desires fellowship with His people; His grace provides the way for them to return to Him.

REFLECTION

Praise God that we're accepted by Him because of the sacrifice and blood of Jesus. We have the assurance of access to God (Heb. 10:19–22), so through Jesus let's continually offer up to Him a sacrifice of praise (Heb. 13:15).

The altar had been made ready for worship in the previous chapter. This chapter continues with details about access to it (vv. 1–3) and those who minister in the temple (vv. 4–31).

The eastern gate is shut because Yahweh had returned through it (vv. 1–3). No one else can access the sacred area of the temple the same way that God had. The permanence of the gate's closure reinforces God's lasting residence among His people (cf. 43:6–7). Nonetheless, the prince can enter the gatehouse to eat a sacred meal before Yahweh.

The theme of restriction of access appears in the next section (vv. 4–14; cf. 43:11). A failure to restrict access within the temple led to worship abuses in the past. Foreigners were allowed to act as guards in the temple (2 Kgs. 11:14–19) but they are strictly forbidden now (v. 9). The Levites, as guards, will bar the entry of foreigners (vv. 10–11). Levites will also minister by slaughtering burnt offerings and sacrifices on behalf of the people. But this is a restricted role because they had been a stumbling-block to the people in Israel's history (vv. 12–13).

Those who were faithful to God, however, are granted the privilege of serving God Himself (vv. 15–31). The Zadokites can access the inner court and offer sacrifices at the altar. This is because of their faithful service in the past (vv. 15–16). They still have to follow certain regulations. There are restrictions on clothing, hair length, the drinking of wine, marriage partners and proximity to corpses (vv. 17–27). Their duties include sacrificing, teaching and judging (vv. 23–24). They are to model what they teach (v. 24). The Zadokites have no landed inheritance; Yahweh alone is their inheritance (v. 28; cf. Num. 26:52–62). Their support comes through the offerings of the people (vv. 29–31).

In short, the Zadokites are to be particularly careful to remain holy because they minister directly before God. The Levites are involved in practical support and maintenance of the temple.

REFLECTION

This division of ministry between those whose service focuses more directly on God and those focusing more on support or practically helping people finds a correlation in the early church (Acts 6:1-6). The Apostles Paul and Peter make a similar broad division in gifting (Eph 4:11-12; 1 Peter 4:10-11). Thank God that He gives His people a variety of different but equally valuable gifts and skills in order to build up His church.

As Ezekiel's final vision (chapters 40–48) continues, the focus shifts to the holy district, the prince and offerings in the new temple.

The landless exiles would be intrigued to find out about land allocation (vv. 1–8). The first priority is Yahweh's portion, the sacred district (vv. 1–5). He is the sovereign landowner, and the centrality of this district emphasises His power and importance. The Zadokites are given land for residence (v. 4; cf. 44:28); the Levites are given land for possession (v. 5). Another portion of land is for the people, perhaps as accommodation during pilgrimages (v. 6). The temple is centrally located, and surrounded by a buffer zone to protect it from defilement. Unlike in the past, the temple is not located in the city but is distinct from it, occupying the central place. On both sides of the sacred district are tracts of land given to the prince (vv. 7–8).

This prince performs the role of a lay leader and represents the worshipping community. His main duty is to provide for the sin, burnt and grain offerings (vv. 17, 21–25), and the people are obliged to bring their harvest and livestock offerings to the prince (vv. 13–16). As he fulfils his role, he is given two warnings. First, he is not to misappropriate people's land (cf. 1 Kgs. 21:1–16); second, he is to ensure the accuracy of the weights and measures used (vv. 10–12).

Regulations are then given for offerings. The sacrifices required to purify the sanctuary and for making atonement are detailed (vv. 18–20). The emphasis on purification is also seen in the Passover regulations (vv. 21–24) and the unnamed festival (v. 25; possibly the Feast of Tabernacles). Maintaining the holiness of the temple (v. 20) and the people (v. 22) is of prime importance.

REFLECTION

God's concern for holiness still continues for us as Christians. We are temples of the Holy Spirit (e.g. 1 Cor. 3:16; Eph. 2:20–22) and God is glorified by the way we live. Let us then strive to live holy lives with God at the centre of all we do, as individuals and as a church.

READ Ezekiel 46

Today we end the tour of the temple with instructions about sacrifice procedures, management of the land belonging to the prince and the temple kitchens.

The prince's involvement in sacrifice procedures continues (vv. 1–15). He also provides offerings for the Sabbath and New Moon festival (vv. 4–6). The priest offers the sacrifice on the prince's behalf but the prince still has the privilege of worshipping Yahweh at the threshold of the inner eastern gate (v. 2). By contrast, the people only have a limited view of the inner court from the entrance to the gate (v. 3). The movements of the prince and the people are regulated (vv. 8–10). The people move either north–south or south–north in one direction. This may be for practical reasons or because the east–west axis was 'holy'.[3]

Regarding the prince's land (vv. 16–18), it can't be given away permanently to someone outside his family because it is an inheritance from God. If the prince passes land to a servant, the land reverts to the prince's family at Jubilee (cf. Lev. 25:13). Again there is a reminder that the prince can't forcibly take the land belonging to others.

The kitchens in the inner and outer courts are then described (vv. 19–24). The kitchens in the inner court are for the offerings that can't leave the sanctity of the inner court (vv. 19–20). Again we see the idea of not transmitting holiness to the people (cf. 44:19). Returning to the outer court, the four kitchens are for the Levites to cook the peoples' sacrifices (vv. 21–23). Even the kitchens maintain the gradation of holiness, protecting the sanctity of the temple.

REFLECTION

At the outer court the people have the privilege of eating in the courts of Yahweh. God wants to commune with His people, a fact which we are reminded of especially in the Lord's Supper (e.g. 1 Cor. 11:23–26). As we feed on the 'body' and 'blood' of Jesus, we celebrate together the new covenant, the atonement and deliverance that we have in Jesus Christ.

DAY 48

READ Ezekiel 47:1–12

Water can be wonderfully transformative, as we see in today's chapter.

As Ezekiel is brought back to the temple, he sees a trickle of water issuing from the south side of the temple, south of the altar, flowing eastward and running through the east outer gate (vv. 1–2). But as it journeys further away from the temple, it becomes a miraculous river. After 450m the trickle becomes ankle deep; then after another 450m it is knee deep; another 450m on, it's waist deep; then finally it becomes a river so deep it can't be crossed (vv. 3–5).

This is a supernatural river. It widens without tributaries and it flows over or through hills and mountains (v. 8). It brings superabundant fertility to a mostly parched wilderness region: fruit trees bearing fruit each month and leaves for healing (vv. 7, 12). It brings healing and life to the Dead Sea, which becomes fresh and teeming with life. This is a blessing to the fishermen from all around the Dead Sea (vv. 8–10). Yet the Dead Sea's production of salt still remains (v. 11). This mineral is useful for seasoning and preserving food, but may also symbolise covenant consummation (cf. Lev. 2:13; Num. 18:19).

What we have is a total transformation of the land, from death to life. The images remind us of the Garden of Eden. In Eden there was a river with four branches, fertile trees and seas teaming with life (Gen. 1:11–12, 20–21; 2:10–14). God will once again bless His people in the land; the Eden-like fertility and abundance they will enjoy flow directly from God Himself.

REFLECTION

This life-giving water anticipates the living water of the Holy Spirit (John 7:37–39; cf. John 4:7–15). Jesus tells us that those who believe in Him receive this wonderful blessing. As Christians the Holy Spirit transforms us and brings to us God's blessings, including eternal life. Yet we, too, can be mini-temples. We can be a source of blessing to the nations by presenting the life-giving message of the gospel (Rev. 22:2).

DAY 49

READ Ezekiel 47:13 – 48:35

As we reach the end of the book of Ezekiel, we picture an idyllic scene where the people can finally be at rest in their own land, with God dwelling among them.

The boundaries of the new Promised Land are first outlined (47:13–23). There are similarities to the boundaries in the original land allotment (Num. 34:1–12). This is the same land that God promised Moses; they receive the covenant promise. Yet radically there is also an inheritance for the resident alien or sojourner (47:22–23). Those who acknowledge Yahweh as their God can enjoy a place among His people (cf. Exod. 12:48; Lev. 22:18).

The next chapter details the specifics of the allocation of the land among the twelve tribes (48:1–29). The dimensions of the portions of inheritance are undefined; only the sacred portion is defined specifically (48:8–22; cf. 45:1–8). The allotment of land among the twelve tribes reflects the original division (47:13–14; cf. Josh. 14–21). The sons of Jacob's wives are closest to the sacred zone (48:4–7, 23–26); the sons of Jacob's concubines are more distant (48:1–3, 27–28). Israel is united again, all living peacefully in the Promised Land.

This unity is reinforced by the gates being named after each of the twelve tribes (48:30–34). The square-shaped city is named not Jerusalem but 'the LORD is there' (48:35).

So the book of Ezekiel ends on this wonderful note. A people in exile look forward to their own portion in the land. A people who felt abandoned by God are reassured that He will be right there among them. It is a word from God designed to inspire repentance, trust and hope.

REFLECTION

As Christians we don't look forward to a landed inheritance. Our rest is salvation in Christ by faith (Heb. 4:1–3). We will inherit the earth (Matt. 5:5). We look forward to our final rest, the heavenly city with twelve gates named after the twelve tribes but with the foundations of the walls named after the twelve Apostles (Rev. 21:12–14). With great anticipation we long for the day when God will dwell right there among us (Rev. 21:22–23). Come, Lord Jesus!

REFERENCES

1 Duguid, Iain M., *The NIV Application Commentary: Ezekiel* (Grand Rapids: Zondervan, 1999), p. 95.

2 Block, Daniel I., *The Book of Ezekiel:* Chapters 25-48 in *The New International Commentary on the Old Testament* series (Grand Rapids: Eerdmans, 1998), pp. 3–5.

3 See Milgrom, Jacob, and Block, Daniel I., *Ezekiel's Hope: A Commentary on Ezekiel 38–48* (Eugene, Oregon: Cascade Books, 2012), p. 212; also see Figure 8 in Block, Daniel I., *The Book of Ezekiel:* Chapters 25-48, p. 573.

MORE IN THIS SERIES

ROMANS
Momentous News
By David Cook
ISBN: 978-1-906173-24-1

MARK
The Suffering Servant
By Jeremy McQuoid
ISBN: 978-1-906173-55-5

DANIEL
Far From Home
By Justin Mote
ISBN: 978-1-906173-68-5

ACTS
To the Ends of the Earth
By David Cook
ISBN: 978-1-909611-02-3

PHILIPPIANS
Press towards the Goal
By Kay Mumford
ISBN: 978-1-909611-31-3

1 THESSALONIANS
Living for Jesus
By Julia Marsden
ISBN: 978-1-906173-67-8

JOHN
Never Thirst Again
By David Cook
ISBN: 978-1-909611-30-6

ESTHER
Silent but Sovereign
By Carolyn Lacey
ISBN: 978-1-909611-84-9

10 Publishing
a division of 10ofthose.com

To place an order call: **0844 879 3243** email: **sales@10ofthose.com**
or order online: **www.10ofthose.com**